TRUE STORY EVENTS

TABLE OF CONTENTS

Pages 1-2

- Introduction....
- My Biography of (Osc)....

Pages 3-4

- Continuing Biography....

Pages 5-6

- Entering High School....

Pages 6-7

- "Getting pulled over" ....

Pages 7

- Last try for graduation test....

Pages 8-10

- "My 5 key points to success "....

Pages 11-13

- Purchase of new car...
- New journal in SC...
- New employee...

Pages 14-15

- "Another shot @ college" ....

Pages 15-17

- "My 5 Key Points to Success"

Pages 20-21

- "Success Journal" ...

INTRODUCTION

Only Success Counts Rehabilitation Center, LLC reflects my very own life. I went through my trials & tribulations and have encounter in making wrongful decisions. Now I've "jumped" on the Road to Success. I'm here to be a mentor & motivational speaker to young individuals & to reconstruct their way of thinking.

MY BIOGRAPHY OF ONLY SUCCESS COUNTS, LLC

What comes to mind when you think about rehabilitation? Rehabilitation is the action of restoring an individual through his/her mental training and therapy after imprisonment or any kind of illness. This involves the mental aspect of the mind when the brain can emphasize the way a person's cognitive activities, physical senses, and emotional expressions. Researcher, Kolbe Corp stated, "Three important parts of the mind are as follows:

Cognitive- This emphasizes thinking such as; IQ, skills, reasons, knowledge, experience, and education.

Conative- a focus on physical traits such as drive, necessity and inmate's forces.

Affective- deals with emotions such as desires, motivation, attitudes, preference, emotions and values.

The desires connected to one's emotional distress can sometimes cause them to exhibit violent outbursts. Many people do not think or rationalize their actions before they commit criminal acts stemming from mental illness, which manifests into situations that oftentimes place them in prison or some type of confinement. As a result, many people do not have access to proper rehabilitative opportunities that can properly help them properly merge back into society. Scientific researcher, Andrew Day, stated "Increasing imprisonment sentences does little to restore an individual's behavior. Longer sentences with less counseling are associated with higher rates of Habitual offender (repeatedly) when the individual return to their communities as the clear majority inevitable do, the problem multiply."

Only Success Count, LLC (OSC) will offer a positive perspective to inform individuals that success comes in many forms and can be achieved at any age.

MY BIO

    Hello, Ladies & Gentleman, I'm Telecka and I'm from a little country town called Hartwell, GA is known for its finest "Lake Hartwell". Introducing my family, I have three big brothers my oldest brother servers his rights in the US Navy, two little brothers and one little sister we were all raised by some good families. My family taught me how to be a respectful, dedicated and reliable young woman. At a young age, I didn't understand the meaning of those mannerly words. Today, I want to inform the young youth of my trials & tribulations and how I went from negative to positive.

    One summer morning, In the year of 2011, I'm having an adventurous dream about being a co-star in the movie Fast & Furious 5. Paul Walker was teaching me the most dangerous stunt jumping my car over one building to the next". My anxiety started to rush & I felt my heart dropping to the floor when the bright sun comes over my house shining through the blinds waking me. I got up and close my blinds not looking at the alarm clock to see what time it was to get ready for school. The house is super quiet that I could hear the birds chirping outside my window. I decided to lay back down and try to close my eyes again for a second but my 6:50 am alarm goes off. My grandmother comes banging on my door stating "Get up and get ready for school. I replied, okay flipping the covers back off me. My feet hit the floor, yawning and stretching my arms. I could smell the hickory bacon sizzling on the stove, eggs & cheese & buttery brown pancakes. I go to the closet to see what's my wardrobe was going to be. I picked out a red & black Polo shirt, black Levi's & black Air Force Ones. Oh, I couldn't forget about my Gold earrings & necklace. After, looking in the mirror checking myself out, I opened my bedroom door beginning to walk to the bathroom to brush my teeth. My big brother Justin was in there taking a shower. I knocked on the door stating, "Hurry up I'm going to be late". He replied, "Man you should've gotten up early and came in here." I was so mad, I replied just hand me the toothpaste and face towel I'm going to go to ma bathroom. When ma is not home she doesn't allow anybody to be in her bedroom. I look at the clock on my phone and it says 7:25 am I must be at school by eight if I want to be counted present. I knew I had thirty minutes to brush my teeth, wash my face and get to school on time. I walk in the kitchen and the good smelling breakfast was waiting on the kitchen table. I grabbed my plate and finish getting ready about to head out the door when I realize I left my books. I turn around to go back in the house to get my books when my homeboy Brot knocks on the door. He yelled, "yo let me catch that ride to school, I missed the bus." As I'm walking to the door heading out I replied "most definitely. "We walk towards the car Brot bust out with a freestyle he yelled "Money on the wall goes crazy" I laughed. Brot & I got in the car about to go when the car wouldn't start. I turned the switch while pushing the gas pedal at the same time when I heard a crying noise. I believe it to be my starter we get out the car slamming the door shaking our heads mad stating "dang man we're going to be late. I figured Brot & I didn't have any choice but to start walking so we did. Hart County High School from my house on Reynolds Street was five miles (15 minutes) apart. As we walking to school we came up to the PJ's on Rome Street when two German shepherds come running our way. We both took off running through Zion Baptist Church coming up in front of Mack's Funeral Home. A red Chevy with green stripes & 22's inch rims comes flushing up the street almost hitting us trying to get away from the dogs. The driver made a complete stop letting down his window mean muggings us by the looks of it he didn't seem happy. My partner Brot looked in the car and said "Lo what's up fool this Lele & Brot boy calm down. "I looked back to see how far the dogs have gotten. They were almost to the car, I opened the passenger car door Brot opened the back door we jumped in and Lo took off. We all laughed so hard about it and I brought up how Brot almost tripped over the sidewalk trying to jump it. Lo asked "where y'all going this time of morning I hope school. I replied "Oh yea education is the key.! "Lo turns his music up loud beating down the block. He had two 12's and amp in the back of his Chevy. Getting to school Lo pulls up in the parking lot letting us out the car at 8:10 am I was late. At the age of 18, I really didn't care about school. All I wanted to do was hang out, party & have money. That was the "Hype" back in high school.

    Attending school wasn't in my biggest plan, four years attending high school, I was a class clown and I didn't take academics seriously. I skipped school, didn't study, turn in homework late and I hung out with the popular kids (mostly the wrong crowd). I used to sneak out of class with my homegirls Rita & Joy we went around knocking on different classrooms doors and run. We did that faithfully and laughed about it in when we have girls talk in the bathroom. In the bathroom talking, I started talking to Rita & Joy about going to college "they replied back" go, man, there isn't nothing else going on down here anyways we about to graduate. "I thought I had it all planned out, I was determined to graduate somehow and go to college. I always was interested in criminal justice coming up. My grandmother & I always got up at five o clock am to drink coffee & watch "In the heat of the night" & Criminal Mind on the weekends. Those shows & long talks with my grandmother positively confirmed that maybe having an interest in criminal justice & going to college wasn't a bad idea. From that moment forward, I made a little change in school & my life. I was more self-discipline I stopped skipping school, I started to study more, I turned my homework in on time and I stop becoming a class clown.

    Four months from graduation approaching, I had to pass all five parts of the graduation test such as Writing, Social Studies, Science, English & Math. One thing about me is I might have been a class clown, but I knew I could be a little smart. It was coming close to the end of the school year, graduation was around the corner. Rita, Joy & Brot have got their test results back stating that they passed all five parts of the graduation test on their third try. I had got my test results back stating that I passed all four parts except for Social Studies on my third try. The passing score for Social Studies graduation test was two hundred I made a one-eighty-nine. I studied and made flashcards to help with the memorialization of Definition, Fill in the Blank & Multiple Choices. I did that every day consecutive.

It was the last day for the retake graduation test, I had so much dedication in passing the test. The last few people were later called to Mrs. Grant the Counselor's Office for their test results. Mrs. Grant stated, at the door to everyone, "if you failed, I'm going to hand you a tissue." But if you pass I'm going to give a smile. My classmate Eric walked in before me, he walked out with a smile saying to me," yea man I passed". I was so nervous but had a little confidence in myself. I was thinking I must pass this test, or I will be embarrassed. I walked in Mrs. Grant office with my head up high. She looked at me, I asked Mrs. Grant did I pass? She didn't say anything but looked at me and gave me a tissue. My heart dropped so quickly to the floor, she said I'm giving you a tissue because you passed! I was so excited, I gave Mrs. Grant a huge hug. Mrs. Grant said congratulations "You Finished What You Started." And I did, I walked out Mrs. Grant office with my head high knowing I was dependable to God, Me & my families. May 25th, 2011 at 7 pm, I walked across the Herndon Stadium smiling from ear to ear thanking God from above for believing in me.

I started to investigate different colleges to apply for. The different schools were Asheville College, Fort Valley State University, Mercer University, and Albany State University. Waiting on a response from the universities Fort Valley State University was the first college to give a response. I entered my freshman year at Fort Valley State University in the fall semester in 2011. The morning of move-in day was a disaster from the jump; First I had to get up at 6 am to be there by 11 am, it was 3 ½ hour drive from Hartwell to Fort Valley & this will be my first time on my own. That early morning my grandma made my favorite breakfast two hickory bacon sandwiches and we started to pack the car with my bags then head to Fort Valley, GA. On our road journey, we stopped by Five Guys known for its famous burgers & fries located in Athens, GA. We took the food to go and while eating, my brother Justin spilled ketchup on the back seat. I was mad because some of the ketchup got onto my new pants. My grandmother stopped by the nearest gas station to fill up and for Justin to clean up his mess. As we pull up at the gas station my grandmother asked me to pay thirty in gas. My brother and I walk into the Exxon Gas Station he walks back to the bathroom for paper towels and I got me a bag of skittles, coke and thirty in gas. After pumping the gas, we landed into Peach County known as Fort Valley, GA. Entering the school gates it was a lot of signs pointing the new students in the right direction to their dorms. I stayed in the commons building seven an all-girls dorm. Unloading my suitcases from the car a Residential Advisor (RA) assists me to the number of my room. Entering dorm number sixteen I meet my new roommate Valerie she's from Conyers's, GA. Valerie was a hairstylist who loves to wear different hairstyles and do people's hair. Both of us were Criminal Justice major students looking for a career in law enforcement. The first day of class I found out I was going to be in learning support. Learning support is an extra-curriculum class such as English, Math, Writing and Reading they are giving to freshman students that cumulate low scores on their ACT or SAT test and it doesn't go towards GPA. The upcoming rule at universities for learning support was only two chances to pass the class final before being suspended for a year. My junior year I was giving two-course to take math & reading. Both classes were deep with fifteen or more students. Mr. Evans was my math teacher he was a hard-up tight teacher who wanted every student to pass his class. Ms. Hill was my reading teacher she was very language correct your sentence teacher. But being alone without any supervision nobody to wake me up for school and no principal calling home I was back on the partying. In the cafeteria on Wednesdays its fried chicken Wednesday with mac & cheese, green beans & corn beard. It was delicious make me believe I was back home eating my mother goods Sunday dinner. While waiting in line for the mac & cheese, I meet Chris, Meat and Fly they all were in college studying different majors. What we all had in common was smoking and partying so that's all we did every day of the week. Our favorite place to party it was the Swamp & Spruce Street them parties used to be lit. I stayed out late with my crew on school nights playing cards and shooting dice at college apartments. I had class the next morning my 7 am alarm clock goes off, I wakened with a major headache from drinking and being up all night. Walking to class I met up with Chris by Moore Hall he was walking to his class also. Chris started talking about the wildlife at the party the night before. Chris. said, "Yo man the party was thick last night & them girls was looking right". I replied, oh yea everybody was turnt!

Arriving at Mr. Evans class he asked did everybody complete their homework assignment chapter 1 through 2 questions in the book? I put my head down because I knew I didn't do any of those assignments I partied instead. Mr. Evans asked the people on the far right to pass down their assignments to the left to get picked up. During class, Mr. Evans stated that the final exam is in two weeks and the scores with be on a scantron sheet. I was nervous in thinking that if I fail both reading & math I will suspend for a year. Class end and I met up with Ashley in the hallway. I tell her how I only have two weeks to prepare myself for the final exam, pass and if not, I will be suspended for a year and I can't go home that would be embarrassing. Ashley stated, man I got to pass writing & reading and if I don't I'm going to get suspended too. I replied, we both in trouble all this partying and no study came to bite us. From that day forward, we slacked up on partying just a little and went more to the library to study for the test. The day of testing I went to both classed with my head up high and gave it my best try. Mr. Evans & Moore gives out each different parts of the test. On each test, we had the time of two hours a total of four hours. I gave it my all and after everybody got finished with their test the teachers ran the scantron through the machine to gives us our final score. Mr. Evans & Ms. Moore split the class up sitting down with every student individually. While on my results I see a lot of my classmates crying due to their results. That there alone had me terrified into thinking I might be in that "go home crew". It was my turn to get my results Ms. Moore gave me a paper with my test score on it. I failed both classes by four points. Ms. Moore stated to me Telecka I'm sorry you were so close but under the university circumstances you will be suspended for a year. I was devastated and embarrassed about failing as a junior.

    Devasted! Walking out of class, I had my head down when I bumped into another student causing his books to fall on the floor. His face expression was furious, I bent down to help him pick his books up. We introduced ourselves with a handshake & smile he introduced himself as Keyshawn. He was a junior also, his major was early childhood education, he wanted to become a 9th-grade science teacher. I told him my major was criminal justice and I wanted to become a homicide detective. He replied, that's cool but not trying to rush you are anything but; I must go I'm going to be late to class homie. Keyshawn runs down the hallway I turn around and start walking out the bonds building walking into Ashley, Chris, Meat & Fly. They were all sitting on the bench talking about how they also failed their tests & being sent home. Chris, Meat & Fly were all from Warner Robins, GA. Warner Robins, GA is a (20 minutes) drive from Fort Valley, GA. I announced that I'm going back home to Hart County. I told them that I'm catch up with them when I come back down this way. We all shook hands and started to walk our separate ways. I try to build my confidence up to call back home and let my family know that I was academically suspended.

    Headed to my dorm, I walked past a group of girls & boys that I knew, and they were smoking, rapping & playing my favorite game (spades). My inner feeling wanted to go over there and join them consequently, I kept walking through my head & hands up greeting the group. I walk inside my dorm sat on the couch huffing & puffing scared to call my family. I take out my phone and start to dial my mother's number, she answers with a hello daughter what are you doing? I replied, oh nothing it's the summer schools out and I'm ready to come home. Ma replied I bet you are Justin will be that way later tonight to pick you up. I said okay and we both hung up the phone, I didn't even get a chance to tell her my devastating news. I went to my room starting to pack my bags and clean out the bathroom. Valerie walks in my room starts talking about how she finished her semester with A's & B's. I was happy for her but at the same time, I really didn't want to hear about someone else success. I congratulate her, and she walks into her room and started to pack. While waiting on my brother Justin to pick me up, I went down to the cafeteria to grab something to eat. After eating my cheese pizza, slurping a strong peach Crush soda my brother calls me stating that he was inside the school gates. I told him that I lived in building 7 and that I was leaving the cafeteria walking back to the dorm. Arriving, at my dorm my brother was waiting outside his car greeted me with a hug. We head back up to my room to grab my belongings and head out. On our road journey to my ma house, Justin mentioned that ma was moving to Columbia, SC for a new job. I replied to him that I was going to move with mom to Columbia, SC for job reasons since I got academically suspended for a year. He replied, well you will be okay just get you a job and go back & when you do, please focus this time. I told that I would, and I wonder what ma going to say about it because everybody was depending on me. He replied, ma going to tell you the same thing but a little more cursing. I was nervous because I still must face her. Meanwhile, we get onto the loop 10 interstate that runs into Athens, GA, and roads that leads to Hart County. We were basically almost at home arriving there at 11 o clock at night. I was so exhausted, I didn't even unpack my bags out the car, I came in and went straight to sleep.

     The next morning, I woke up to my ma & grandma cooking breakfast my favorite Hickory Smoked Bacon, eggs and toast. While sitting at the table having breakfast I announced that I will be home for a year I got academically suspended. My ma & grandma food almost came out of their mouths when I said that. My ma said what? What happened? My grandma said the same thing. I looked at both of their faces and both faces were staring at me like they were on a set for a horror movie. I repeat it and start to tell them not everything about (partying, drinking & smoking) but now I wasn't focused and had the same drive as I did in high school. I request a roommate to my ma (humorously) to move in and get a job in Columbia, SC. Ma replied a course you can move with me but Telecka you must do damn better and stop smoking and focus on your work! I replied, that I completely understand, and I will. I ask when you are moving she said I already have starting moving somethings I only have to get the rest of my clothes because I'm going to buy new furniture later. I was back excited for a second knowing that I have a better environment living in another state with my ma.

Starting my new journey in Richland County in Columbia, SC was bittersweet. I was leaving my loved ones, my brother and grandmother. The very next day I got up and started to look for jobs on Craigslist. I came across Amazon Fulfillment Center in Cayce, SC it was off exit 11B about (20 minutes) from ma house. I applied for the job and was contacted back by email asking me to come in for a drug & skills test. I quickly called my ma and told her that I have a job interview and I need a car to get back & forth to work. She was so happy that only a day of me being in Richland County I got an interview. Not even a day later, my ma boyfriend at the time came across a white 1996 Nissan Sentra it was 800 dollars with no tax. I called my daddy mother and asked her could she go half with me on my first car, she replied that she would. I had her to send it through Western Union and I picked the 400 dollars up on the same day. After getting all the money together my ma and her friend took me to Advance Auto Parts parking lot where the car was advertising. Walking up to the car there was a phone number on the driver's window referring call for sale. I get out my I-phone call the number and asked about the car facts & test driving. The owner stated that the car was her youngest daughter car that she had in her high school days. Also, she stated that the car is 800 upfront and I can most definitely test drive it. I said awesome I'll wait here at the auto parts store. The owner pulls up with a girl in the car gets out introducing her as her daughter who once drove the car. She also meets my ma and her friend. We get in the car and start to test drive it. We head on the I-95 interstate and drove to the next exit when I tell my ma that it drives wells and I want it. She said okay you got! We drive back to the auto parts where the owner & her daughter were and make my first car purchase. The first stop I made in my new car was Goo's car wash. It clearly had "wash me" written on the back window I wanted to purchase the triple foam wash which often comes as red, gold and blue colors. Triple foam products come as conditioners or polishes. Goo's is an automatic pay & wash company that customers pay their money into a kiosk machine. The customer must put their car in neutral & ride automatically through the car wash. Riding through the car wash I see wonderful colors cleaning the outside of my car the chemicals were (these neutral or acidic products condition and prepare the vehicle's clear-coat to accept sealant and protectant products as well as expedite the drying process). Reaching the end of the tunnel, the automatic kiosk required me to stop, wait & go. I pull into an empty parking space to clean and vacuum my car out. I also clean my tires and rims with awesome spray and tire shine foam. After getting my car clean, I drove back to my ma house to show them my car (before & after). I walked into the house smelling some fried pork chops sizzling on the stove. I enter the kitchen where my ma was cooking bacon mash potatoes on the stove along with Jiffy butter biscuits. I really couldn't wait for her to finish cooking I was ready to eat right then. While waiting on the food to finish, I came across reminding my ma that I have a job interview in the morning. She replied I remembered now you have a way to your interview not only that but back & forth to work. I replied, yes mother I already claimed this job when I received the email. Fingers crossed and saying my prayers that this could be my big break. My ma announced the food being ready so my ma, her boyfriend & I sat down at the dinner table to eat our delicious food. After eating everything that was cooked my belly was completely full I could barely get up from the table. I finally get up to clean the crumbs off the table and put my plate in the dishwasher. I go get ready for my big day in the morning I take a bath, get my clothes out and organize my notebook with my resume. I jump in my queen size bed to get some shut-eye I've had a long exciting week I was exhausted!

The next morning arrives I was wakened by the cold air blasting from my vent above my bed. I get up with sinus problems nose and throat stopped up. Furthermore, I had an important interview today, so I had to get well to go. I ran out of my room into my ma room crying because I couldn't breathe. I jumped on her bed pleading for quick working medicine. She gave me some Allegra. I took the medication with a glass of water and I stayed in the house and bed all day until two prior to my interview. Getting myself together for the interview was a drag due to my illness. I honestly believe I would wake up in full effect without the stuffiness. Unfortunately, I still must proceed into making my good first impression on the interviewers. I go to my closet and pick out my professional outfit which was light Levi's, brown belt and yellow with a black horse polo shirt with black loaves. I check myself out in the mirror grab my notebook and walk out the door getting into my car. Excited that I have a CD player already in my car I started to bump Rocko "this morning I wake up feeling like money". Reaching exit 11B the sign to Amazon Fulfillment Center was right off the exit. I reached the guard shack giving the guard my name to check the entrance list. I get through the gates arriving fifteen minutes early. Eventually, I get out my car organize & spray cologne on my clothes. In addition, I walk into the front door greeted by the security officer addressing me to the right room. The interview line was full of many genders in and out of the room. Consequently, we were giving order number to speed up & keep down the confusion. While waiting almost twenty minutes I was finally called for my interview. Before I walked in I fixed my clothes once again, said a quick prayer and remembered to keep it short & simple. In the interview room, there were two current employees' sitting at the table with many papers with questions on them. I greet myself as Telecka and the two employees introduced themselves as Monica & Jessica. Their (1) question was "why do you think you're the perfect candidate?" I replied I'm the perfect candidate that puts safety first. The (2) question was "what are your skills?" I replied I can drive forklift, word, excel, PowerPoint and lift 60lbs. Monica & Jessica gave me a fantastic look and asked would you be interested in being a cherry picker for 2nd shift Sunday through Wednesday 5 pm to 5:30 am four days out the week. I rush and replied with a yes ma'am I can start immediately. That following Sunday night I started my first day as an Amazon employee. My first day on the job the new employees were told that we have an agenda meeting before the shift starts every day. The agenda meeting was basically about what goal is for that day & how we can reach them. During the meeting, the supervisor introduced the new employees to the present employees. The supervisor grouped us up with this woman employee who've been there for 7 years they called her aunt bee. Aunt bee was a blunt, loudmouth, a keep it real person that we made an instant connection. Aunt bee showed me how to be the best cherry picker I can be. A cherry picker description is an employee that works by themselves pick items by the product number that appears on an RF gun. After picking the items box, tape and label them, then place them on the conveyor belt. I worked at Amazon for 10 months before I realized that I needed to finish what I started. Therefore, I told my ma that I was going back to school to continue my education but this time I'm going to start at a technical college to help me academically. She replied, I'm so proud of you to finish what you started baby, you save some money up to go back down to Warner Robins, Ga and make a difference. I honestly felt the wisdom that my ma was preaching to me, so I did, I started to apply at Central Georgia Technical College which is concurrent with Fort Valley State University.

In the year of 2015, I got my first apartment & also got accepted into the Criminal Justice Program at Central Georgia Technical College located in Warner Robins, GA. I started school in the late fall and yes, I dropped down from a university to a technical college but, I met some good wonderful educated men's (twins) name Anthony & Antonio Sears. Both the Sears brothers were my Criminal Justice Instructors. They taught me to realize while in school take it seriously and to set high expectations for yourself. Unfortunately, having my own apartment with no supervision or RA I sort of feeling back into making the wrongful decision. I used to have parties, cookouts, and sleepovers about every day of the week. My neighbors would complain about the loud music and the smoking that they use to threaten to call the police. But being young and wanted to be accepted I didn't care about going to jail. My instructor Antonio use to catch me coming to class high and I use to deny it. He also uses to tell me by the people I hung around going to get me caught up. At the age of twenty-one in 2014, My homeboy Gary & I went to chill with some girls and smoked (Marijuana). We were heading home on Houston Lake Road being the only car on the road at 3:30 am. We get to the red light when the police got behind us. Turning onto Corner Street the police car pulls us overturning on his warning lights (red & blue) along with sirens sounds. I stopped the car telling Gary I think I'm going to jail. He replied "Man chill we are going home. "The officer was taking a little minute getting out his car I was nervous because the myth says when a cop takes long to get out the car "sometimes" that means you're going to jail. After five minutes he finally gets out the car and walks right to the driver's window. I let my window down waiting on him to ask me for my licenses &

Insurance Card. He says, "license & Insurance Card please." I reach in the glove department and pull out my wallet and gives him my information. The officer walked back to his car closed his door and looked up my information. While waiting on the officer to return I'm talking to Gary about the suspicion of the officer. Gary replied, "Chill man we good, we don't have nothing." The officer walks back to the driver's side window I let the window down the officer says "Ms. Johnson I'm going to have you to step out the car for me. "I stepped out the car nervous because I didn't know what's about to take place. He asked to have I been smoking in my car. I replied "No sir ". He said I smell marijuana coming from your person. I told him that I have smoked earlier. The officer flashed the lights on my eyes to see were they dilated. After checking my eyes, the officers tell me that he wants me to do a DWI test which was; hold my head back with my right leg up at the same time. Walk with your heel to heel back & forward nine times and count to twenty backward (Mississippi style). After doing all the procedures he placed me under arrest. I asked him why I'm getting arrested he replied, "You failed the test." I fussed and argued with him about being able to drive home safely. He read me a pamphlet stating to take a drug test, I refused so I was charged with DWI (which is DWIs and DUIs are usually defined as driving while impaired by alcohol or other legal or illegal substances. BAC of .08% or higher.), Gary was arrested also. I was devastated because I never had a record before or got to any trouble. The day of court, I was charged with DWI, twelve months on probation, forty-hours of community services to get done in six-month, a Fine of fifteen-hundred & I had to meet my Probation Officer every-two weeks for a random drug test. Gary & I did our community services at the golf course picking up golf balls all day for about four hours. If we stayed the four hours he would give us six, an extra two hours. I was motivated to complete my community services sheet and turn it in. In addition, I realized criminal justice wasn't going to be my density with that DWI on my background.

    After getting turned down from many jobs I knew a change had to be made. I quit smoking got me a good decent job and pray that one day I can have a clean slate again. Six months into probation, I was working at Bluebird Manufactory Plant in Fort Valley, GA. Bluebird Manufactory makes school buses & other bus companies from the ground up. I'm talking real hard labor work six days a week working twelve hours a day in the heat. But most of all the company pays good money $12 hour. One hot summer day working at Bluebird I was on my thirty-minute lunch break with my co-worker Brian when I receive a call from my probation officer Tasha. Officer Tasha told me today was my lucky day, I asked her how she told me in addition, the judge reduced my charge to City Ordinance which means not a crime, I got off probation less than twelve months, I only paid Six-Hundred in fines and finally the judge ordered to sign the document to restrict it off my background. God has been so good to me. All these wonderful successful assignments were happening all at once it seems like.

I got to experience an extern at Sentinel Probation. Also, I attended the Warner Robins Citizens Police Academy and graduated with a certificate. In May 2017, I graduated with my Associates Degree in Criminal Justice at Central Georgia Technical College. What I learned from my negative experiences is to stay motivated always. One memo I will never forget says "Getting into trouble is EASY but getting out is HARD."

MY 5 KEY POINTS TO SUCCESS

- Dedication
- Determination
- Motivation
- Self-Discipline
- Dependable

SUCCESS POINT 1
(Determination)

Create Positive Vibes: With a positive atmosphere, you will think of everything as possible. You will learn to convince yourself that nothing will ever be impossible.

Set Up Your Self Confidence: Self-confidence lets you face the challenges and give you more willingness to implement your plans to succeed.

Strong Mindset: Being focus and concentrated with achieving success is as important as those two factors explained earlier.

SUCCESS POINT 2
(Self-Discipline)

Acknowledge Your Weaknesses: Too often people either try to pretend their weaknesses don't exist or they try to minimize the negative impact their bad habits have on their lives.

Establish a Clear Plan: Whether you want to increase good habits – like exercising more often, or you want to eliminate bad habits – like watching too much TV, you'll need to develop a plan to outline the action steps that will help you reach your goals.

Visualize the Long-Term Rewards. Visualize yourself meeting your goals and reaping the rewards that you'll gain by practicing self-discipline daily.

SUCCESS POINT 3
(MOTIVATION)

Hang Around with Positive, Motivating People You become the like the people you surround yourself with.

Communicate in a Positive Way: A simple rule is to use positive communication to help the motivational forces within you. Choose to smile.

SUCCESS POINT 4
(DEDICATION)

Desire: You can't achieve anything that you really, truly don't want to achieve.

Determination: You can't achieve anything without having the *courage* to step out of your comfort zone to pursue your goal.

Discipline: You must step away from motivation and emotions. Train yourself to do whatever it takes in a controlled and habitual way.

Devotion: You must love what you do. Enthusiasm for your goal is a driver to keep going.

SUCCESS POINT 5
(DEPENDABLE)

Manage Commitments. Being reliable does not mean saying yes to everyone.

Start and Finish. Keeping your word or simply doing the right thing is rarely convenient, so reliable people let their actions rise above their excuses.

MY MEMO OF SUCCESS

S-Success

U-Utilize

C-Communication

C-Completion

E-Education

S-Separation

S-Self-Discipline

    The moral of this story is to persuade the young youth from being negative to positive. Through all the trials & tribulations I went through as a youth, I honestly can say it was a rough and depressing moment in my life. Without believing in myself and putting God first I would've made it. Finish what you started and watch how your future blossom. Thank You!

THE SUCCESS JOURNAL

During my trials & tribulations I begin to write down in my success journal what I need to work on. From that movement forward, I started checking off what I have accomplished.

Writing down your problem looks better on paper! The success journal will help bring your success to light.

<u>Improvement</u> & <u>Success</u>

Improvement & Success

Improvement & Success

Improvement & Success

LLPRINCE
(BROT)

Made in the USA
Middletown, DE
22 May 2022